To my parents, Arthur and Celeste Lewis, who must have found it difficult to have a daughter who questioned everything and yet believed in the impossible.

To my sister, Jamie Lewis, who, by looking up to me, gave me a reason for living up to an ideal.

To my children, Charles Wareham, Christin Von Musser and Lara Lewis, the treasures of my life.

To Beverly Green, who came up with the concept and the wonderful idea of using the ABCs, and who gave me ideas, feedback, editorial help and encouragement.

D0596598

The ABCs of Life

From Women Who Learned The Hard Way
by Beca Lewis Allen

World Leisure Corporation
Boston, MA/Hampstead, NH

Distributed to the trade in USA by Login Publishers Consortium,
Chicago; tel. (312) 733-8228, (800) 626-4330.
In Canada by General Publishing Co., Ltd.; tel. (416) 445-3333.
Distributed to giftstores by Sourcebooks, Inc., Naperville, IL;
tel. (800) 798-2475; (708) 961-2161.
Mail Order, Catalog and Special sales
by World Leisure Corporation, Boston;
tel. (617) 569-1966, fax: (617) 561-7654

ISBN: 0-915009-35-8 (12-book prepack ISBN: 0-915009-36-6)

The ABCs of Life

INTRODUCTION

This book began with a request from my youngest daughter.
She often called me from college to ask advice for herself and
her friends. Finally, she asked me to write it all down, and
voilà! A book was born.

Most of this advice grew out of observations from my own
life. Though it was often filled with soap-opera-type plots,
I discovered that in the end, it is not the ride that counts,
it's what you walk away with. I have walked away with
a heart filled with gratitude for my children, who took the
ride with me, and my friends, who were there to support me.
Thanks to all of you, but specifically those
who helped make this dream a reality:

To my mentor, Dorothy Hardy, and my friend, Candy Romine Belasco, who demonstrated to me their model of unselfish love.

And to my best friend and husband, Carl Allen, whose honesty, directness, loyalty and love fill me with awe and give me courage.

Do not indulge in what is not good,
but rejoice in all that is!

The ABCs of Life: Part I

The ABCs of Love

HOW TO RECOGNIZE AND KEEP A GOOD MAN

Acknowledge your man as often as possible.
Tell him how wonderful he is to you.
Pick something good about him to focus on,
no matter how small.
He has to start somewhere.

Beware of a man who is just getting over
another serious relationship.

Count out a man who is abusive physically, verbally or emotionally. In his case, the words "I love you" are abusive, too. Leave.

Discover your man's values and honor them as if they were your own.

Enjoy your life when he's not around.
He loved you for the life you had
before you met, so don't stop now!

Forget a "Mommy's Boy."

Give up a man who spends all his spare time
"hanging with the boys."
He will not grow out of it just because you
came into his life.

Hold on to a man who knows that behind
every good man there is a good woman—
and who LOVES it!

Involve your man in your life.
He needs to know he is valuable to you.

Justify his trust in you. Never betray him in
thought, word or action.

Keep a man who knows that behind every good woman there is a good man, and he is willing to be that man for you.

Let a him be a man, and you be a woman.

Make sure you realize that once you sleep with a man, you have lost your ability to think objectively.

Never give a man an ultimatum.
You will lose! Give him enough valid
reasons to do what you want, and he will.
Don't tell him, show him.

Observe his actions. They speak louder than
words. Observe your actions.
Make sure they match what you say.

Parenthood is an important issue.
Be sure your man shares your views on this subject.

Qualify a man's intentions.
Remember: Even the best of them has one goal—Sex.

Run from a man who has been to hell and has decided to wallow in the experience. *That's all he will ever be able to do. He won't be able to make a commitment to his own progress in life, let alone yours.*

Split from a man who thinks everything is someone else's fault, especially yours.

Treasure a man who has been to hell
and who CAME BACK.

Understand that a man
will always "look."

Value the time a man spends with you. Time
is his greatest gift, so don't waste it by
whining about what he does wrong.

Want a man who has learned how to put his relationship with you first.

X-rate your past love life. This is for only you to remember. Just tell him he is the best (and make it true).

Y*earn to understand first and to be understood second.*

Z*ero in on a man who loves to love you well.*

BEING A WIFE

Ask about all joint finances. Become part of the decision process. If you are in charge of finances, make sure your husband is part of the decision process.

Be careful not to turn the words "husband" and "wife" into job descriptions.

Create a home environment that will make
   him love to come home.

Don't fence yourself or him in.

Establish credit in your own name, not just
   as a tag-on to your husband's account.

Find someone you can completely trust to talk to if your marriage is not working.

Grow wiser together.

Have a savings account in your name that you don't tell him about.
Save consistently.

If a fight occurs, never bring up old issues, and never call him names or label him.

Jokes made at each other's expense are not funny.

Keep intimacies and secrets sacred. They should stay only between the two of you.

Learn about what interests him most so you can talk about it intelligently.

Make a wonderful marriage a priority. It will be a strong and consistent base for everything else that either of you does.

Never blame each other for anything. State the problem and find a way to solve it together.

Open your heart.

Plan exciting things to do together,
each week, month, year, and
far into the future.

Quietly and consistently view your husband as
the most wonderful man in the world. Treat
him as such, and watch what happens!

Refrain from including your best friend in everything you and your husband plan. He may be tempted to make plans with her himself.

Set a weekly "date" night, and keep it.

The only way to keep your man is to give him freedom to be himself.

United you stand, divided you fall.
Heal all divisions immediately.
Keep an eye out for the small and subtle
ones, as they are the most dangerous.

Veto any thought of withholding sex as
punishment, or using it as a reward.

Withdrawing in any way is a slow and
certain death to a relationship.
Keep communicating!

X & O's. Your kisses and hugs may not be
acknowledged at first, but they are seeds
in a garden. Eventually they will produce
flowers.

You can spend hours on the phone with
your girlfriends when your husband is not
home. When he is home, make him your
priority, so he can make you his.

Zap the belief that once you are married,
you don't have to look good.
Become more beautiful, both inside and
out, with each passing year.

BEING AN EX-WIFE

Analyze what you did wrong the first time and don't do it again in your next relationship.

Be careful when dating a new man. If he is nice to you, you might think this is love.

Cultivate interests you kept on hold while you were married.

Drop all comparisons between your ex-husband and your new love.

Explain to your children, in a way that they can understand, everything that is going on. Don't keep it a secret — they will know something is happening and they'll invent their own scenarios.

Forgive your ex-husband for what he did wrong. Not forgiving keeps the pattern in your life and it will show up again with someone else.

Get excited about what the future offers.

Hanging onto "what ifs" keeps you chained to the past. The key is self-forgiveness. That was then, this is now.

If you are still in his life, be a true friend to his new wife.

Join a support group.

Keep your friends.
*These are the people who love and
support you no matter what man is in
your life.*

Let him go.

Make sure that your children are very clear that they are not the cause of the divorce.

Negotiate terms in your divorce that do not make you a victim now or in the future.

Organize your assets. Be sure to transfer them to your name.

Practice safe sex.

Qualify new men in your life carefully.
*It may be wise to have them investigated
before starting a serious relationship.*

Redecorate your old home, or decorate your
new one, to reflect your personal style.
*This time you don't need to make any
compromises.*

Say nice things about your ex-husband to your children. They need a father they can look up to.

Take time to know yourself.

Understand clearly what you want next time, and don't settle for less.
Choose qualities in a man that match your values.

Vitalize your look! Remember, the best revenge is looking good.

When he remarries, don't interfere.

X-husbands are a learning experience, not a life sentence.

You are wiser than you were before. Treasure that wisdom, and use it.

Zillions of accusations will never make the past right. Leave the past out of any current discussions you have with your ex-husband.

PLEASING A MAN

Asking if he loves you is telling him that he has failed at showing you.
Actions do speak louder than words.
Appreciate what he does.

Be aware that his greatest fear is that if he loves you, he will lose himself. Help him see that loving you means he can be more of himself.

Clutching, begging and being moody most of the time are three sure ways to lose a man.

Discuss *what is important to you when your emotion over the issue has faded into the background.*

Everyone *wants to be allowed to be happy. Men are no different.*

Feeding *a man is the way to his heart. But you don't have to cook the meal.*

Give clear hints when you want sex.
Men can't tell.

Honor him and your relationship.

If you feel you **must** say it, **DON'T!**

Just saying, "Oh, nothing," when he asks what's bothering you, could be interpreted as a rejection. Tell him as much of the truth as you can.

Keep negative thoughts to yourself.

Let him do things for you, and be grateful!

Men are simple to figure out.
*They just want to know you will always
let them be men.*

Nothing *pleases a man more than knowing
you want to please him.*

Okay, *sometimes he wants you to wear
short skirts. Wear them and enjoy the
attention.*

Physical actions, like washing your car, are his way of saying, "I love you!"

Quell your desire to be a know-it-all, even if you do. Keep quiet and let him find it out for himself.

Realize that a man doesn't like to be rejected and often will not make the first move. Make it clear that when he asks, you won't say no.

Surprise him with small useful gifts. Even if he says he doesn't like surprises he'll love this kind — and you.

Take him to places he has never been before. Plan everything yourself so he can feel pampered.

Understand that very few men want to marry a woman who has slept around a lot, but they do want a woman who is unafraid and experienced in bed. Get it?

Verbalize your love.

Want to discuss something important?
Take him out to eat.

X-ray your motives before you do anything
that may jeopardize the relationship.

Yield when necessary.

Zing him with your happiness because he is around.

The ABCs of Life: Part II

The ABCs of a Career

BEING A STUDENT

Attend your graduation and buy a school ring.

Break bad habits now, before you accept them as part of your character.

Call your parents.

Discover the value and joys of the library.

Enjoy every minute of school.
   It will be a time you will remember with
   pleasure the rest of your life.

Find a self-defense class and take it.

Get your newly made friends' addresses when you leave school. Keep in touch.

Help new students get acquainted. Introduce them to your favorite places and people.

Ignore anyone who says you can't.
*If it is something you are impelled to do,
find a way and do it.*

Join a school organization.

Keep the catalogue of your school's classes. You
*will need the course descriptions later if you
go back to school or transfer.*

Label your clothes so they don't get mixed up in your roommate's laundry.

Make the acquaintance of the Dean of your college.

Nominate yourself to something that brings out your talents.

Own a Swiss army knife with lots of attachments and keep it with you.

Plan your school career with the help of a guidance counselor.

Quiz yourself as you study.

Remember, the purpose of school is to get an education and to learn to think.

Stay in school.

Take a variety of courses. In the process you might find your life's passion.

Understand how the system works, and make it work for you.

View good study habits as money in the bank and free time in your life. Learn them and use them.

Watch your eating habits. Start eating healthy now. You'll learn more, look better and live longer.

Xerox copies of all your school records. *You'll need them again someday.*

Yes, you can — and should — ask for help *from your teachers when you need it.*

Zone out occasionally. *Take a break to take care of your emotional needs.*

GOING ON A JOB INTERVIEW

Absorb everything asked of you and practice your responses for the next interview.

Bring a resume that is tailored to the job for which you are interviewing.
If you need help writing a good resume, get the book *The Damn Good Resume Guide by Yana Parker.*

Comment on something that interests you about the interviewer or the items in his or her office.

Don't bring up anything unflattering about
your past unless you are asked about it.

Echo the interview questions by rephrasing
them before you answer.

Forget wearing perfume that day.
Your interviewer may be allergic to it,
or it may remind him of someone.

Give several reasons why hiring you
will produce the results the company is
looking for.

Habitually send thank-you letters
as soon as possible after the interview.

Initial impressions are hard to overcome.
Make yours outstanding!

Juggling a briefcase and a purse can be difficult. Try carrying just a briefcase.

Know your strong areas and promote them. If you are asked about your weaknesses, show how you are overcoming them or turning them into assets.

Let them know clearly what YOU can do for THEM. Remember, you are unique.

Mentally review possible questions and the answers you will give.

Never, never be late!

On corporate interviews, take the conservative approach with dress, hair and makeup.

Practice your handshake. A firm handshake conveys confidence and competence.

Question the interviewer regarding how he or she envisions your role in the company, then explain how you can fulfill that vision.

Research the company before you go on the interview.

Scope out how people dress at the company and dress that way, top of the line.

Try on your new outfit before you go, so you will look and feel comfortable.

Upgrade the image you have of yourself.
If asked if you can perform a certain task,
even if you are uncertain, say yes.
Then take a class or get help so you can.

Volunteer information only about your work performance. Keep your personal life to yourself.

Wear your best lingerie. It will help your morale.

X-out the loud or chunky jewelry.

You can make a great impression with a company by impressing the receptionist first with your sincerity and professionalism.

Zip through a typing or computer skills test by practicing before you go on the interview.

ON THE JOB

Always write down the name of the person
on the other end of the telephone line.
You may later need to verify the
information they gave you.

Break down tasks and do them one step
at a time, top-priority steps first.

Cut down the time you hang out at other people's desks.

Do the job the way they ask you to do it, and do it well. After that, you can show them a better way.

Earn the respect of your coworkers and boss by being efficient.

Find a way to enjoy every job you do.
*In order to make things change, you must
be grateful for what you have.*

Gossiping will label you as "one of the girls."

Have a sense of urgency when working
on a project.

Improve your value by taking outside
   classes.

Jump at the chance to do a project that looks
   too hard.

Keep a jug of good water at your desk.
   It will keep your desire for coffee and
   munchies at bay.

Look *for a mentor and gratefully learn all you can from that person.*

Motivate *your staff by first finding out what motivates them.*

Never *have an office romance with the boss. If you must, find a new boss first.*

Offer to do what you know how to do. Otherwise, your talents might go unnoticed.

Pretend this is your own business — Someday it might be.

Question everybody about their jobs and how each one fits into the whole picture.

Resolve to not believe anything you hear about co-workers unless they tell you themselves.

Study all advances in your field.

Take time to see whether your job is moving you toward your long-term goals, and what you can do to improve the situation.

Undertake the task of writing a manual for your position. This will make it easier to train someone to take your place so that you can move up in the company.

Valuable information can be learned by being the person who is listening, not talking.

Write down the skills that you learn and file them. This may help jog your memory when you write your next resume or a proposal for a raise.

X-hibit a cooperative attitude at all times, at least outwardly. When you can no longer approach your job with enthusiasm, perhaps it's time to find a new job.

You can plan for future opportunities by networking with people at other companies who work in your field.

Zip your lip before you give personal
information to co-workers.
*You never know how it might come
back to haunt you.*

OWNING YOUR OWN BUSINESS

Always do "tasks for cash" first in the business day.

Be an expert at what you do.

Create relationships. This in turn will create business.

Determine whether you want to create a market or cater to an existing one.
This one decision will affect what kind of business you choose.

Educate yourself as to how big business and markets work. Use the information to your advantage.

Find a way to take time off. Your business doesn't own you, you own it, remember?

Get expert advice and take it.

Hire people who know things you don't
know, and can do their job better than
you can. Then help them do it.

Inventory your values and make sure your
business is in harmony with them.
Otherwise, if you succeed it may be at the
expense of things you believe in.

Join and become active in organizations
that support women and your business.

Keep the vision of why you are in business
in the forefront of all business decisions.

Love doing what you love to do.

Make your reputation synonymous with
your business.

Negotiate all your deals with the idea that everyone must benefit.

Offer to write articles about your field of expertise. This is a great way to become known as an expert. If you don't write well, find someone who does and collaborate.

Put together a sound marketing plan and evaluate its performance monthly.

Quietly build a network of people that can provide you information or help at a moment's notice.

Return calls as soon as possible. Callers may be in the minor leagues today, but tomorrow could become major league players — with a long memory!

Sell when you are at the top.

Tell your clients how your product or service can help them, and then give them even more than you promised.

Understand that the best way to inspire your staff is to stay inspired yourself.

Value yourself, your talents, and your time. If you don't, then neither will anyone else.

Wear the best shoes you can afford. Many people judge your status by your shoes and how you take care of them.

X-out any client that undermines you or your business.

You are promoting your business in everything you say, wear, or do. Make sure it is always excellent.

Zealously pay attention to details.

The ABCs of Life: Part III

The ABCs of
Family Relationships

DEALING WITH PARENTS

Acknowledge *their contribution to your life.*

Break *away if necessary.*

Communicate *anything that has been bothering you so that it can be resolved if possible.*

Develop your own self-image.
You are not just your parents' child.

Evaluate what you learned from them,
then decide what is useful and what is not.

Forgive them for what they did
or did not do. This way, you can
get on with your life.

Get your mother or father to write down
the recipes for your favorite dishes.

Help them plan for their future.
If their future is not carefully planned,
it may become yours.

Investigate your heritage.

Joyfully hug them hello and goodbye.

Keep them up-to-date with what your children are doing. Allow them to be important in your children's lives.

Let them know what you love — or like — about them.

Make an effort to get to know them. Find out what their lives are like when they aren't being parents.

Next time you visit, hide a present for them. One day when you would like to be there but can't, you can tell them where to find it.

Often parents really know what they are talking about. Listen to what they mean and don't debate the words; you may hear their wisdom.

Parents are people, just like you. The day you really understand this, you have grown up.

Question your parents about their childhoods. Record or videotape the discussion.

Realize that a mother's or father's love can, and often does, come from people other than your parents.

Share your hopes and dreams with them. It's possible that they will help you achieve them.

Take videos of your family throughout the year. Make it your Christmas or Hanukkah present to your parents.

Unearth their secret dream and help them accomplish it.

Verify what you remember from your childhood by asking them now, while you still can.

Write down what you would do differently as a parent, then do it. If it doesn't work, you can always do what they did.

X-out the need to make your parents proud of you. Be proud of yourself.

You will enjoy your parents more when you give up how you wish they had been, and see them instead for what they are — and be grateful for it.

Zealously send cards, notes, and letters, especially on special occasions.

BEING A MOTHER

A *well-rounded child is a happy child and will become a happy adult.*

Be *prepared to grow up yourself.*

Create traditions. In times of great change, these are the things that children can count on.

Demonstrate to your children what love looks like so they have a model for loving others.

Educate your children to love education.
Reading to them is a great first step.
Turn off the TV and provide lots of books.

Find a way to give clear guidelines
for what is expected of them.

Give your children reasons to do well.
Physical punishment is not a good reason.
Logical explanation helps them make
good decisions when you are not there for
them to fear.

Help your children discover what is special
about them.

In no time at all, your children will be grown. Make time for them now!

Just remember: how you let your sons treat you when they're young will be exactly how they treat other women when they grow up.

Keep your word or explain logically why you cannot.

Listen to your children before you jump to conclusions. They may be right.

Making your adult children choose between you and their spouses will never make you happy.

Notice good behavior and reward it. *Give bad behavior a quick reprimand, but do not dwell on it. All they want is attention — give it to them for the right reasons.*

Once you are a mother, always be a mother first.

Put "happy notes" into their lunch box.

Quietly and gently guide. Lead by example.

Remember, you have until they are three years old to teach them what love feels like, and until age five to teach them their value and the value of others. If they have learned these two things by then, they will have a solid foundation.

*S*ew visible hearts onto the backs of their clothes so they can tell front from back, and at the same time be reminded you love them.

*T*he greatest gifts you can give a child are guidelines for behavior and the ability to be independent.

Underline the necessity for them to assist anyone who is less fortunate.

Value their desire to be independent. Setting them free is the only way to keep them.

Write a yearly letter to each child. Save the letters until your child's 18th birthday, and present them as a collection.

X-out any negative statements to or about your children.

Your children cannot live the life you wish you had. They are here to live their own, so help them.

Zero in on what makes them happy and find a way to help them achieve it.

BEING A STEPMOTHER

Act as if you belong there. You do.

Be equal in the treatment of your children and his.

Compliment your husband on his children.

Don't make your spouse choose between you and his children. You will lose, whichever choice he makes.

Establish a daily routine that everyone can count on.

Find a way to have quiet time with your husband with no children around.

Give them an opportunity to go to a camp each summer so they have time to develop, away from family expectations.

Help their mother stay in touch. Send her pictures and schoolwork. Remember, it's what you would want if the situation were reversed.

It's true that you cannot and should not
   take the place of their mother,
   but you are their parent.
   Step up to the plate and be one.

Look for everything wonderful in your
   stepchildren, then tell them what you find.

Make a point of listening and understanding your stepchildren. Then you can ask them to understand you.

Notice what doesn't work and correct it immediately.

Obtain a "medical permission" from their mother in case of an emergency.

Plan family outings in which everyone can participate.

Quench any desire to tell your stepchildren in anger, "You're just like your mother."

Respect your husband's wishes regarding his children. If you don't agree with him, discuss it out of sight and hearing of the children.

*S*tay true to who you are, so your stepchildren can get to know and love the real you.

*T*ake the time to attend school events and visit their teachers. Let them know you care about their lives and their future.

Understand that your stepchildren may be
slow to demonstrate their love for you.
Decide that it's unimportant,
and just love them.

Verify any messages sent through the
children from their mother.

What makes you a parent is choosing to
act like one.

Xmas and other holidays should not be a time when children must choose between those they love. Make it easy for them. If necessary celebrate your holidays on a different day.

You must be sure you are willing to be a stepparent before your marriage.

Zigzag your way through the mine fields of stepparenting with grace. Your reward will be the knowledge of a job well done, and the gratitude and respect of your husband.

BEING A GRANDMOTHER

Allow yourself to become a legend to your grandchildren. Be someone they can tell all their friends about.

Be your grandchild's best friend.

Celebrate that you are a grandparent.
What a gift!

Delight in the fact that the best part of your
life is now.

Encourage all your grandchildren's dreams
and be their advocate.

Find a way to be with them for holidays
   if possible.

Give gifts to your children on their
   children's birthdays.

Honor your grandchildren's individuality.

Interfere in the raising of your grandchildren
only when their mental or physical safety
is in jeopardy.

Juggle your life so you can be with your
daughter when your grandchildren
are born.

Know that being a grandmother is
a state of mind, not an age.

Let your children know how well they are doing with their children, and how proud you are of them.

Make up for what you couldn't do for your children by helping them now with theirs.

Never betray your grandchildren's trust. When they tell you a secret, keep it a secret.

Offer your grandchildren what they need most: someone who will listen to them.

Put away money for your grandchildren's futures. An education fund will be one of the greatest gifts you can give them.

Quench your grandchildren's desire to know more about their parents by telling positive anecdotes about their parents when they were young.

Repair any breaches in communication as quickly as possible.

Support the guidelines your children have set for their children. *If you must disagree, do it in private.*

Take them places they would never be able to go on their own.

Undertake the task of putting your estate in order.

Videotape yourself telling the family history. Give copies to your children and grand-children.

Welcome the fact you once again have "children" in your life, now that you know so much more about how to enjoy them.

X *marks the spot where your treasure lies—in your family. Share your wisdom and love with them every chance you get.*

Y *ummy treats are always grandmother territory.*

Z *oom to their rescue when they need you.*

The ABCs of Life: Part IV

The ABCs of Living

STAYING HEALTHY

Always think health first. Without it nothing else is the same.

Be creative about exercise. It doesn't need to look like it does on television.

Cutting out any one of the three components of exercise—aerobic, weight resistance, and stretching—is like having a three-legged stool with two legs.

Dining out is a pleasure, not an excuse.

Eat small amounts of food all day. This keeps your metabolism running. It is when it slows down that what "passes your lips stays on your hips."

Find your own way of eating that keeps you healthy, and stick with it.

Gravity has a harder time affecting toned muscles.

Have a partner in health. The goal is to encourage each other to do better and not to agree with each other's excuses.

It's ridiculous to work hard to become rich, but ignore your body to the point you don't like the way you look. Money can't buy self-esteem any more than it can buy health or love.

Joints get stronger when you require them to work.

Keeping old habits narrows your options. Get rid of them and be free to make new choices.

Listen to your body. If you haven't heard it for awhile, it may take some practice.

Mental health and physical health cannot be separated.

Never eat a heavy meal within two hours of going to bed.

Overeating, smoking and drinking are health thieves. Don't give up your greatest wealth—your health—to a thief that has no power except what you give away.

Push away your plate before you finish your meal. Which is cheaper, wasting food or paying to get it off your body?

Quickly take care of any health problems. *Putting them off does not make them go away.*

Resolve always to take care of your health first.

Snacking isn't bad, it's what you snack on and when.

Trying to control desires only makes them stronger. Observe and disown them, without judgment or guilt, and they will dissolve.

Unkind words to yourself about your body only makes the problem worse.
Learn to love your body! As soon as you love it, you will take better care of it.

Verify all advertising claims before you fall for a new health fad. Someone wants you to buy because they make money when you do.

When you get older you need less food. Accept it and eat less.
Think of it this way: Now you have more money to spend elsewhere!

X-out the habit of rewarding yourself with food. Pick a more productive reward.

You have only so many calories per day to spend. Determine your calorie budget and spend it wisely.

Zesty thinking produces zesty living.

AS TIME PASSES

As friends and family become older and
wish to pass on, respect and honor their
wishes and let them go when it's time.

Be flexible.

Check to be sure that the life and health insurance policies for you and your spouse are adequate for your current needs, and those of your loved ones.

Decide not to count birthdays.
Want to celebrate a special day?
Count trips around the sun.

Exercise is not an option. It is a necessity.

Find something new to learn and become an expert at it.

Getting older is not an excuse for anything.

Hang out with young people.
Feeling young is a state of mind,
not an age.

Ignite a fire in your best friend and
do something exciting together.

Jealously guard your time. Don't waste it
on unimportant things.

Keeping the pains and regrets of the past is the primary cause of aging. Rewrite the past or forget it.

Love everyone and everything, but most of all yourself.

Make the most of every moment of every day.

Notice that you feel old only when you notice that other people are getting older. *Stop looking at age.*

Occasionally update your image to keep up with the times.

Plan pleasures and trips for many years in the future.

Quit talking about old age and its problems. *You will just make more of them.*

Realize that you probably will live longer than your mate. Plan together for your welfare and you will be able to remember him in peace and with love. Seventy-six percent of women who were married will die as widows.

Saying "No, I can't" will age you faster than the years. Saying "Yes, I can" will turn back the clock.

There are many physical problems associated with aging that can be avoided. Stay fit and you'll head them off before they can take root.

Understand that advertisers make money selling you the idea of old age and the products you'll need. You don't have to play along.

Variety is the spice of life. Pick one new thing to do each week, or change the way you do something now.

Wisdom: Use it, don't collect it.

X-tra attention should be paid to all the friends that you have collected through the years. If you don't know where they are, find them.

Youth is only wasted on the young if you don't claim it for yourself.

Zoom in on all the desires that you have put on hold, and do them.

PERSONAL PLEASURES

Allow yourself to hire someone to clean your home.

Buy flowers for yourself.

Cultivate a garden or house plants.

Dance! Dance at home, go out to dance or take a dance class. It works like magic.

Eat your favorite food — often!

Find a great masseuse and
get a body massage.

Get a great haircut
— one you'll want to keep.

Hot water, bubbles and candlelight
will restore your peace.

Imagine yourself in your favorite sanctuary, whether real or imaginary.

Jump at the chance to go shopping. Buy something special for someone you love.

Kick your shoes off and get a foot massage.

Light a fire and cuddle up by it.

Manicures and pedicures are an inexpensive way to feel like a million bucks.

Nourish your mind by attending a play, class or lecture. They will broaden your perspective.

Occasionally sit in a steam room, sauna or Jacuzzi.

Purchase something, no matter how small,
that reminds you how wonderful you are.

Question everything you don't understand,
and even some things you do.

Read a good book.

Stroll through the woods, a garden or an open-air market.

Take naps.

Update your clothes with new accessories.

Volunteer for a charity or political cause.

Write a list of everything you do that makes you happy. Next time you're depressed, pick something off the list and do it!

X-*out time in your date book to spend only on yourself.*

Y*oga is great for the body, mind and spirit. Try a class for a great stress reducer.*

Z*ip down to the nearest makeup artist and get a makeover.*

LIFE IN GENERAL

Allow more time than you think you need — for everything!

Be kinder than you think is necessary.

Create learning and growing opportunities for yourself.

Dry clean all pieces of an outfit at the same time — even if you didn't wear each piece. Dry cleaning solutions vary and may alter the color of the fabric.

Expect miracles to happen ALL the time. Find the good in everything.

Feel grateful for everything you have.
It will open doors to more.

Go with your gut feeling, especially if it
conflicts with the message you're hearing.

Have a good attorney as a personal friend.

Introduce yourself by stating your first and last name. *This has much more impact than your first name alone.*

Joyfully live each moment of the day.

Keep a memory box.

Let someone know where you are at all times, for safety's sake.

Make your physical health and your financial health your number-one priorities. Learn how to take care of your body and your investments.

Now is the time to do the things you have dreamed about. There may not be a tomorrow for them.

Once in a while, be outrageous!

Put everything into perspective and keep your priorities straight.

Quickly pay off all your debt.
Don't use debt for anything that doesn't
produce a return.

Research and practice the customs of any
country you are planning to visit.

Stay current on technology.
The age of technology and information
is here to serve you.

They can't step on you if you don't lie down.

Understand what lifestyle you want.
All your decisions should be in concert
with that choice.

Vote. If you don't vote, you have no right
to complain.

Write in a journal on a consistent basis.

X-hibit good taste in all you do and say.

You can create a dramatic entrance when you enter a room by pausing and then walking into the room confidently.

Zealously do what is practical,
but live as if anything
is possible.

ABOUT THE AUTHOR

Beca Lewis Allen received her Master's Degree in Dance
from UCLA, and ran a successful dance school and
dance company. She currently lives in Los Angeles with
her husband, Carl Allen. Together they own *Allen's Body
Art*, a health and fitness company. Through her
company, *The Shift*, she teaches classes, and speaks on
paradigm shifts and the power of perception. She also is
a Certified Financial Planner
and licensed stockbroker.